RICH TOWARD GOD

A Study on the Parable
of the Rich Fool

© 2024 by FaithFi: Faith & Finance, LLC
All rights reserved.

No portion of this book may be reproduced, stored in a retrieval system, or transmitted in any form or by any means—electronic, mechanical, photocopy, recording, scanning, or other—except for brief quotations in critical reviews or articles, without the prior written permission of FaithFi: Faith & Finance, LLC.

Readers should be aware that Internet websites mentioned as references or sources for further information may have changed or may no longer be available since this book was published.

ISBN (Softcover Trade Edition)
979-8-9894556-0-7

Scripture quotations, unless otherwise noted, are from the ESV® Bible (The Holy Bible, English Standard Version®). ESV® Permanent Text Edition® (2016). Copyright © 2001 by Crossway, a publishing ministry of Good News Publishers. The ESV® text has been reproduced in cooperation with and by permission of Good News Publishers.

Author: Carolyn Calupca
Content Director: Chad Clark
Creative Director: John-Mark Warkentin
Cover design: John-Mark Warkentin

Special Sales
FaithFi resources are available at special discounts for bulk purchases. For more information, please contact us at orders@faithfi.com

Printed in the USA

23 24 25 26 – 10 9 8 7 6 5 4 3 2 1

1st Printing

FAITHFI.COM

@FAITHFIOFFICIAL

Download the FaithFi app available for iOS and Android

WELCOME

The team here at FaithFi is delighted to bring you the *Rich Toward God* study. We have chosen to explore the Parable of the Rich Fool from Luke 12, not because it presents an easy lesson, but because it asks a fundamental (and even difficult) question: "Am I living a life that is rich toward God?"

Following Christ is often called "the Christian walk" because living as a Christian is supposed to be a forward-moving, life-encompassing journey. The biblical financial principles we teach every day on the *Faith & Finance* radio program, online, and in the FaithFi app, are just a part of the picture. Spiritual disciplines such as studying God's Word, participating in Christian fellowship, serving others, and sharing your faith are also essential elements in the life of a maturing believer.

This study is another tool to help you expand your understanding of God's amazing love for you and what it means to follow him with all your heart. Our hope is that a closer walk with the Lord will lead you to a deeper understanding of what it means to be truly rich in your faith. The joy of serving God and others as a faithful steward makes so much more sense when you realize the extent of God's grace in your life.

Thank you again for joining us in this journey of faith through the study of Luke 12:13-21. Our prayer is that you will *"know the love of Christ that surpasses knowledge, that you may be filled with all the fullness of God."* (Ephesians 3:19)

In Christ,

The FaithFi Team

TRUTH & BEAUTY

At the genesis of time, God's Word and breath initiated life in all of its variety, goodness, and esthetic beauty. At FaithFi, we believe God's true Word still takes center stage, and the use of beauty and creative storytelling is God's age-old method for bringing his message to life for the contemporary church.

01

In this study, we draw a connection between 1st-century Jewish barns and our contemporary American grain silos. You'll find Jesus' parable in Luke about the wealthy farmer and his barns quite relevant in today's context.

02

The cover cut-out in the form of a silo also serves as a window into the book, a window into the parable, and ultimately a window into the heart of the reader. *"For where your treasure is, there your heart will be also."* (Matthew 6:21)

Author: Carolyn Calupca
Content Director: Chad Clark
Creative Director: John-Mark Warkentin
Editor: Jim Armstrong
Editorial Review: Michael Blue, Luke Bolton, Sharon Epps, Rob West
Layout Design: Matthew Anderson
Printing & Logistics: Kevin Light

03

The use of abstract geometric shapes allows us the flexibility to expand the metaphor of grain to represent the various ways possessions can captivate and own our hearts.

Our hope is that God's Word, through the power of his Spirit, will free you to live lives rich toward God because your hearts are captivated by the true treasure.

Typefaces:
Martina Plantijn by Klim Type Foundry
Resonanz B by Out Of The Dark Type Foundry
PP Mori by PangramPangram Type Foundry
New Spirit by Newlyn Type Foundry
Paper: Soporset Coverx Smooth White

HOW TO USE THIS STUDY

This study can be used by individuals, couples, small groups, and churches.

Familiarize yourself with the Introduction and Historical and Biblical Context before you begin Week 1. It will help you focus your thoughts throughout the study.

Before you begin each week, ask God to reveal himself to you through his Word.

Enjoy each week's study with suggestions for Scripture meditation and questions to help you dig deeper into God's Word.

    Questions to help you better understand Scripture.

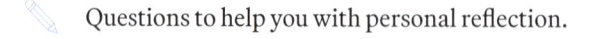

    Questions to help you with personal reflection.

> **For the Word of God is living and active, sharper than any two-edged sword, piercing to the division of soul and of spirit, of joints and of marrow, and discerning the thoughts and intentions of the heart.**
>
> HEBREWS 4:12

To help you apply what the Lord is teaching you, each week is broken into the following sections:

Setting the Scene
What is the biblical context?

Digging Deeper
What are the scriptural principles that need to be understood?

Recap
What are the main points?

Reflect
What did I learn about myself and God?

Pray
How can I talk about this with God?

Practice
How can I apply what I learned?

Completing this study may take longer than four weeks, and that's okay. Please take the time you need to experience the full benefit of your time in God's Word.

Table of Contents

Introduction — 11

Week 1 — 17
True Abundance
LUKE 12:13–15

Week 2 — 37
Pride in Prosperity
LUKE 12:16–18

Week 3 — 57
The Uncertainty of Tomorrow
LUKE 12:19–20

Week 4 — 83
Rich Toward God
LUKE 12:21

Continue the Journey — 103

Introduction

In the beginning, God formed man and woman in his image. He created them to enjoy everything good that he made, for fulfilling work, and relationship with himself. Tragically, rebellion and sin separated humankind from the Lord, leaving us with only echoes of Eden.

Whether we know it or not, we still desperately want and need God, but worldly impulses tempt us to seek fulfillment of our desires for happiness, well-being, and prosperity in misguided ways. Advertisements and media encourage us to pursue the things of this world, and a sense of entitlement and self-love pervades our culture.

And yet, in the midst of temptations and worldliness God is at work, as he always has been. His plan from the beginning was to reveal himself to humanity and redeem his creation. Right this minute, he loves you more than you can imagine, and he wants you to know him better. We pray that the Holy Spirit will draw you into a closer walk with Jesus through this study of God's Word.

In the following pages, you will find a four-section study on the Parable of the Rich Fool found in Luke 12:13-21. This study provides a deep dive into God's Word, encompassing the themes of greed, treasure, pride, and abundance.

At the conclusion of the parable, Jesus calls his disciples to be "rich toward God." This is the central question of this study: What does being "rich toward God" look like for us?

Surely it doesn't mean making God rich. He doesn't need anything.

Could it mean getting rich yourself and then being generous?

Or perhaps being rich toward God is about doing good deeds, as in Matthew 5:16: "*Let your light shine before others, so that they may see your good works and give glory to your Father who is in heaven.*"

So, what does it really mean to be rich toward God?

May the Holy Spirit use this study in his Word to lead you to an answer and, in the process, to a deeper relationship with the Lord.

Follow along as Jesus teaches on the plains of Judea: a memorable parable about a very rich man with a very big problem.

The Parable of the Rich Fool

¹³ Someone in the crowd said to him, "Teacher, tell my brother to divide the inheritance with me." ¹⁴ But he said to him, "Man, who made me a judge or arbitrator over you?" ¹⁵ And he said to them, "Take care, and be on your guard against all covetousness, for one's life does not consist in the abundance of his possessions." ¹⁶ And he told them a parable, saying, "The land of a rich man produced plentifully, ¹⁷ and he thought to himself, 'What shall I do, for I have nowhere to store my crops?' ¹⁸ And he said, 'I will do this: I will tear down my barns and build larger ones, and there I will store all my grain and my goods. ¹⁹ And I will say to my soul, "Soul, you have ample goods laid up for many years; relax, eat, drink, be merry."' ²⁰ But God said to him, 'Fool! This night your soul is required of you, and the things you have prepared, whose will they be?' ²¹ So is the one who lays up treasure for himself and is not rich toward God."

LUKE 12:13–21

Historical and Biblical Context

It is about 33 A.D., and Jesus, completing his third year of ministry, is walking to Jerusalem for the last time. He has crisscrossed the country in the usual fashion of itinerant rabbis, but in his case, the crowds following him number in the thousands (Luke 12:1). And no wonder. *"He was teaching them as one who had authority, and not as their scribes."* (Matthew 7:29)

For three years now, the Spirit of the Lord has been empowering Jesus to *"proclaim good news to the poor...to proclaim liberty to the captives and recovering of sight to the blind, to set at liberty those who are oppressed, to proclaim the year of the Lord's favor."* (Luke 4:17-20) It's hardly surprising that people are drawn to him.

The crowds seem to be most impressed by the miracles Jesus performs. They follow because wherever Jesus is, people get fed, both literally and spiritually. Jesus has been healing the sick, casting out demons, even raising the dead. Who wouldn't be compelled to take their own needs to Jesus and see how he might speak to them?

Jesus' teaching of the Parable of the Rich Fool comes near the end of his earthly ministry. Many times in these last days before his trial and death, Jesus addresses the hearts of his followers, warning about persecutions and judgment to come, and admonishing them to turn from sins that impede their relationship with God.

The Gospel of Luke

Luke, a physician, is writing *"an orderly account"* (Luke 1:3) of the life of Christ for his Gentile patron, Theophilus. Luke had not been one of Jesus' twelve disciples. Yet, Luke was a diligent student and had closely followed the accounts of those who spent many years with Jesus, including eyewitnesses to his life such as Mary, the mother of Jesus.

The Gospel of Luke includes more parables than any other gospel, and the Parable of the Rich Fool is only found in Luke. Parables are a common rabbinical teaching tool, using familiar scriptural themes and real-life situations to point to spiritual truths.

Jesus uses this form of teaching to reveal truth about God's kingdom to those with spiritual insight. On the other hand, those who refuse to believe Jesus' teaching continue in their spiritual ignorance, not understanding the real meaning behind the parables:

> "Because seeing they do not see, and hearing they do not hear, nor do they understand."
>
> MATTHEW 13:13

Week 1

True Abundance

LUKE 12:13–15

TEACHING PASSAGE

¹³ Someone in the crowd said to him, "Teacher, tell my brother to divide the inheritance with me. ¹⁴ But he said to him, "Man, who made me a judge or arbitrator over you?" ¹⁵ And he said to them, "Take care, and be on your guard against all covetousness, for one's life does not consist in the abundance of his possessions."

LUKE 12:13–15

Setting the Scene

Imagine yourself in the crowd with Jesus that day. It's hot and dusty, and the throng has swelled into the thousands. People are shoving and *"trampling one another"* (Luke 12:1), trying to get closer to Jesus. Will he cast out another demon? Heal someone's leprosy? Or maybe criticize the synagogue leaders again? Of course, nobody has handed you a bulletin that says, "Today, Jesus will teach about the Parable of the Rich Fool," so you really don't know what will happen next. You just feel there's something momentous brewing, with this remarkable teacher at the center of it all.

As he travels in the area, Jesus teaches his close disciples and the crowd. He admonishes them to repent and encourages them to live attentively with God in mind.

A group of religious leaders, including Pharisees and teachers of the Law, is also following along. Most don't seem to believe the words of this Galilean teacher, and they want to limit his influence among the people. They pepper him with questions, trying to catch him in some blasphemy in order to discredit him. Some of the religious leaders are so threatened by Jesus' claims to be the Messiah that they are planning to have him killed.

There is tension in the air. Rumor has it that Jesus is heading to Jerusalem, where the political and religious pressures are escalating. Some believe he is going to Jerusalem to proclaim himself king. Others fear that if he enters the city, his enemies will attack.

Meanwhile, Jesus has paused in his public teaching, addressing a few words of encouragement and warning to his disciples (Luke 12:1-12). Suddenly, someone steps forward and asks him to intervene in a family dispute: *"Teacher, tell my brother to divide the inheritance with me."*

Digging Deeper

Rabbinic law, based on Deuteronomy 21:17, ensured that each son would inherit equally at the death of a parent except the firstborn, who inherited a double share. This "birthright" represented the firstborn's status as leader of the family, responsible for carrying on the father's legacy. This is why Esau's selling of his birthright in exchange for dinner back in Genesis 25 was so significant. Esau essentially rejected his responsibilities as the eldest son. For the sake of his appetite Esau relinquished his inheritance to Jacob, who then became the "father" of the clan of Israel.

Jesus' listeners understand the importance of birth order and inheritances, and it is common for disputes about these issues to be settled by rabbis. In this instance, Jesus refuses to take the case, saying, *"Man, who made me a judge or arbiter over you?"* Jesus sees into the heart of the questioner, as he zeroes in on the real issue—covetousness. Or, in our terms: greed, materialism, and selfishness.

Warning Against Covetousness and Greed

After speaking directly to the inheritance-seeking brother, Jesus cautions him and the crowd with these words:

> "Take care, be on your guard against all covetousness, for one's life does not consist in the abundance of his possessions."
>
> LUKE 12:15

Re-read Luke 12:15.
Circle the words that stand out to you.

> Take care, be on your guard against all covetousness, for one's life does not consist in the abundance of his possessions.
>
> LUKE 12:15

How is this speaking to you personally?

The word *covetousness* refers to a greedy desire for worldy gain or a longing for someone else's possessions. In the context of this parable, Jesus is warning against desiring material possessions to the extent that all other priorities become twisted out of proportion. This is a sin in which God takes a back seat to the desire for accumulating material things.

Most of Jesus' audience are probably not rich, so you might think they are more prone to coveting other people's wealth. Or you might think he is aiming his teaching at the preoccupation of the rich with accumulation and display. But Jesus doesn't distinguish between the rich and the poor. He knows everyone can fall prey to thinking that their desires for "life" can be fulfilled by having more stuff (or having someone else's stuff). Greed and covetousness are sins that distract us from God as we longingly gaze at what others around us possess.

Covetousness, as described in the Old Testament, is such a danger to the human heart that God warns against it in the Tenth Commandment:

> "You shall not covet your neighbor's house; you shall not covet your neighbor's wife, or his male servant, or his female servant, or his ox, or his donkey, or anything that is your neighbor's."
>
> EXODUS 20:17

The New Testament speaks strongly against the sin of covetousness, too. Here are two examples:

> For you may be sure of this, that everyone who is sexually immoral or impure, or who is covetous (that is, an idolater), has no inheritance in the kingdom of Christ and God.
>
> EPHESIANS 5:5

> Put to death therefore what is earthly in you: sexual immorality, impurity, passion, evil desire, and covetousness, which is idolatry. On account of these the wrath of God is coming.
>
> COLOSSIANS 3:5-6

Take a moment to close your eyes, calm your thoughts, and go to God in prayer.

Ask the Holy Spirit to reveal the material things you might be coveting and write them down.

What desires are behind each of these things?

"Keep a strict hand on your own hearts, lest covetous principles rule and give law in them."

— MATTHEW HENRY

Jesus admonishes his followers to "*take care, and be on your guard against all covetousness.*" The Greek word for "take care" can also mean "consider" or "beware," indicating this is a warning. According to Matthew Henry's commentary, the second charge, to "be on your guard," means "keep a strict hand on your own hearts, lest covetous principles rule and give law in them." Jesus is warning us to protect our hearts diligently against a takeover by covetousness and greed.

How can you protect your heart from greed and covetousness?

Redefining Abundance

Jesus follows up his warning against covetousness with a startling statement—both in his time and in ours— *"one's life does not consist in the abundance of his possessions."*

This countercultural statement begs the question: "If material abundance isn't what makes life satisfying and full, what does?"

Here's what Jesus says about this:

> "I am the door. If anyone enters by me, he will be saved and will go in and out and find pasture. The thief comes only to steal and kill and destroy. I came that they may have life and have it abundantly. I am the good shepherd. The good shepherd lays down his life for the sheep."
>
> JOHN 10:9–11

In this passage Jesus declares his identity as both the door and the good shepherd and his purpose as the bringer of abundant life.

- What does Jesus do for those who "enter by me"?

- The good shepherd lays down his life for the sheep. Why is that so important?

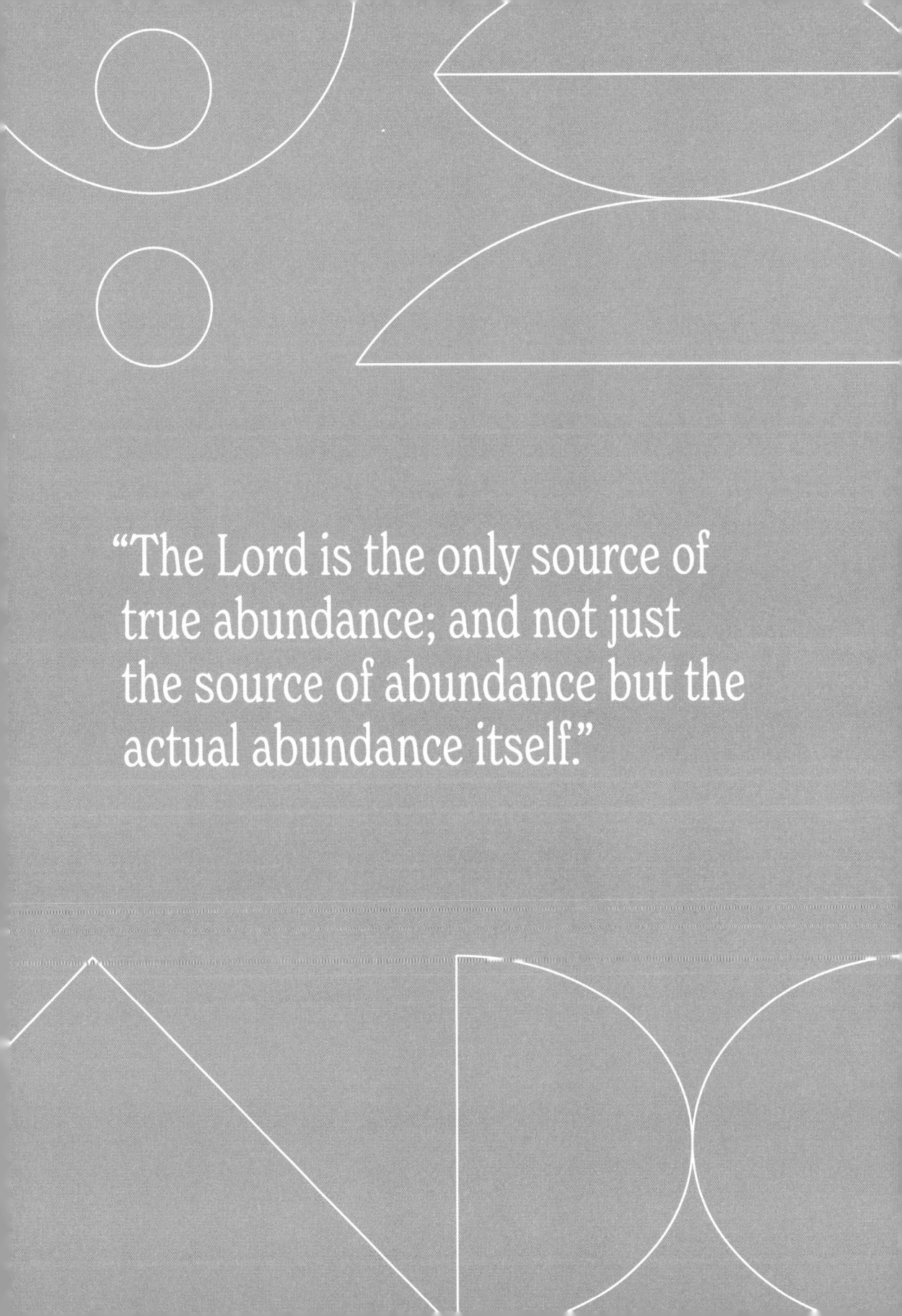

"The Lord is the only source of true abundance; and not just the source of abundance but the actual abundance itself."

The Lord is the only source of true abundance; and not just the source of abundance but **the actual abundance itself**. Throughout the New Testament, and specifically in the Parable of the Rich Fool, Jesus urges us to take the focus off "me" and "my stuff" and put it where it belongs—on Him. Jesus wants his followers to absorb the truth that their abundance comes from a personal, intimate relationship with him:

> "Whoever abides in me and I in him, he it is that bears much fruit, for apart from me you can do nothing."
>
> JOHN 15:5B

What does it mean to abide in Christ and how does that lead to an abundant life?

Recap

- Jesus is traveling to Jerusalem for the last time before his crucifixion, followed by a crowd of thousands.

- A man steps out of the crowd and asks Jesus to settle an inheritance dispute.

- While refusing to take the case, Jesus uses the question to address the heart of the matter—*covetousness*.

- Jesus issues a warning in Luke 12:15: *"Take care, and be on your guard against all covetousness, for one's life does not consist in the abundance of his possessions."*

- Abundant life is not found in what we own, but in the person of Jesus, who came so that we *"may have life and have it abundantly."* John 10:10

Reflect

Take a moment to meditate on the following questions:

What have you learned about God from this week's study?

What have you learned about yourself?

Pray

"Heavenly Father, thank you for your Word, which is living and active, sharper than any two-edged sword. By the power of your Word and your Holy Spirit, cut away any covetousness in my heart, and forgive me for attaching my desire for life to worldly things rather than to you. Teach me how to live abundantly in Christ. In Jesus' name, Amen."

WEEK 1 — TRUE ABUNDANCE

Practice

Here are a few activities to help guide you
as you meditate on this week:

Write down two practical ways you can abide in Christ and direct your attention toward an abundant life in him. Try them this week and see what happens.

Make a commitment to read Psalm 23 as you start each day this week. As you meditate on this familiar psalm, reflect on the ways the good shepherd leads you into abundant life. Keep a journal of your thoughts as the Lord leads you through.

PSALM 23

[1] The Lord is my shepherd;
I shall not want.
[2] He makes me lie down in green pastures.
He leads me beside still waters.
[3] He restores my soul.
He leads me in paths of righteousness
for his name's sake.
[4] Even though I walk through the valley of the
shadow of death, I will fear no evil,
for you are with me;
your rod and your staff,
they comfort me.
[5] You prepare a table before me
in the presence of my enemies;
you anoint my head with oil;
my cup overflows.
[6] Surely goodness and mercy
shall follow me
all the days of my life,
and I shall dwell in the house
of the Lord forever.

Week 1 — Journal

Week 2

Pride in Prosperity

LUKE 12:16–18

TEACHING PASSAGE

¹⁶ And he told them a parable, saying, "The land of a rich man produced plentifully, ¹⁷ and he thought to himself, 'What shall I do, for I have nowhere to store my crops?' ¹⁸ And he said, 'I will do this: I will tear down my barns and build larger ones, and there I will store all my grain and my goods.'"

LUKE 12:16–18

Setting the Scene

In traditional rabbinic fashion, Jesus turns a real-life circumstance into a teachable moment for us. In last week's passage, we met a man hoping to resolve an inheritance dispute by asking Jesus to hear his case in front of the crowd. Instead of gratifying the man's desire, Jesus uses a parable to expose the ways that greed and covetousness separate people from God. Before he starts into the parable, he makes a profound statement that challenges his followers as it challenges us: *"One's life does not consist in the abundance of his possessions."*

Jesus then proceeds to introduce us to a rich man who has everything most people dream about, materially speaking. He's rich, owning land that continues to produce "plentifully." Farmers in the crowd know how hard it is to reap consistently abundant crops, but this man has prospered to the point that he has run out of space to store his surplus. You can imagine the "wishful thinking" going on in the minds of the people around Jesus as he paints this picture of wealth and success.

Digging Deeper

In this week's passage, we get a glimpse into the mind of the "rich man." His financial affairs have prospered, and he finds himself facing a dilemma: His wealth is expanding, but his storage space is not. He seems to be in an enviable position of material abundance.

📖 Describe the rich man's attitude toward his increasing wealth.

📖 Re-read the passage, looking for the ways this man is self-focused. Circle the words *I* and *my*.

> ¹⁶ And he told them a parable, saying, "The land of a rich man produced plentifully, ¹⁷ and he thought to himself, 'What shall I do, for I have nowhere to store my crops?' ¹⁸ And he said, 'I will do this: I will tear down my barns and build larger ones, and there I will store all my grain and my goods.'"
>
> LUKE 12:16-18

📖 How many times does the man refer to himself?

In spite of his uncommon wealth, the rich man's anonymity makes him a kind of "everyman," and we begin to see ourselves in him. He goes to great lengths to accumulate, protect, and relish his possessions, depending on them for satisfaction, status, and security.

📖   The rich man has a problem. What is his solution?

Think of the effort and cost that would be required to tear down all his existing barns and build new ones. It would be like tearing down your house and rebuilding it to add closet space, or buying a bank to safeguard your suddenly overflowing bank accounts.

📖   Why do you think he chooses such a drastic solution?

In what ways do you work to increase and preserve your material possessions?

What role, if any, do you think community and wise counsel play in helping us overcome selfishness and self-reliance?

The Love of Money

The rich man evidently believes his security, hope, and joy are connected to his abundant possessions. That's why he goes to such great lengths to protect what he has accumulated.

But to what purpose? As King Solomon points out in Ecclesiastes 5:10-12, money cannot ultimately satisfy. In fact, Solomon, who was the richest man in the world at the time, called the love of money "vanity," which can also mean "frustration" or "futility."

> [10] He who loves money will not be satisfied with money, nor he who loves wealth with his income; this also is vanity. [11] When goods increase, they increase who eat them, and what advantage has their owner but to see them with his eyes? [12] Sweet is the sleep of a laborer, whether he eats little or much, but the full stomach of the rich will not let him sleep.
>
> ECCLESIASTES 5:10-12

How does the reality of Ecclesiastes 5:10-12 compare with the expectations of the rich man in Jesus' parable?

"He who loves money will not be satisfied with money, nor he who loves wealth with his income; this also is vanity."

ECCLESIASTES 5:10

By clinging to the belief that his wealth will bring life, the rich man becomes a slave to his growing possessions. In Matthew 6:24 Jesus refers to this form of slavery when he warns that we cannot serve two masters. We cannot serve both God and money.

Oswald Chambers, writing in his classic devotional, *My Utmost for His Highest*, concludes that the only solution to such bondage is redemption in Christ:

*"When you yield to something, you will soon realize the tremendous control it has over you. Even though you say, 'Oh, I can give up that habit whenever I like,' you will know you can't. You will find that the habit absolutely dominates you because you willingly yielded to it...**But yielding to Jesus will break every kind of slavery in any person's life.**"*

The rich man in Jesus' parable has wholeheartedly and unrepentantly yielded to his money and possessions. He is holding tightly onto his things and is seeking his future satisfaction from them.

Boasting in Riches vs. Boasting in the Lord

The rich man in Jesus' parable never acknowledges God's blessing or authority in his life and treats his abundance as if it's completely his own doing. He does not recognize that God is the one who holds his physical well-being and security in his hand.

In the Old Testament, Jeremiah rebukes Israel for having a similar arrogance, pride, and self-satisfaction. Because of their sin, he prophesies God will intervene in their story with a season of captivity and exile to call them out of their heart slavery. But Jeremiah also gives God's rebellious people a prescription for reconciliation and abundance. He spells out what it means to live out their beloved identity as those who can know and be known by God:

Thus says the Lord: "Let not the wise man boast in his wisdom, let not the mighty man boast in his might, let not the rich man boast in his riches, but let him who boasts boast in this, that he understands and knows me, that I am the Lord who practices steadfast love, justice, and righteousness in the earth. For in these things I delight, declares the Lord."

JEREMIAH 9:23-24

Use Jeremiah 9:23-24 to fill out the table below.

Do not boast about...	God's people should boast about...

What is the rich man in Luke 12 boasting about?

In light of Jeremiah 9:23-24, what does God offer the rich man (and us) to boast about instead?

Describe a situation or times when you might be tempted to boast about something you did or something you have.

How could remembering God's steadfast love, justice, or righteousness lead you to respond differently?

In 2 Corinthians 10:17-18, Paul echoes Jeremiah's admonition to boast in the Lord:

> "Let the one who boasts, boast in the Lord." For it is not the one who commends himself who is approved, but the one whom the Lord commends.
>
> 2 CORINTHIANS 10:17-18

Ultimately, all credit for our achievements and accumulations belongs to the Lord. He made us, provides the gifts and abilities that enable us to work, and by his grace promises us a relationship with himself that satisfies more than any material blessing.

> For from him and through him and to him are all things. To him be glory forever. Amen.
>
> ROMANS 11:36

"For from him and through him and to him are all things. To him be glory forever. Amen."

ROMANS 11:36

Recap

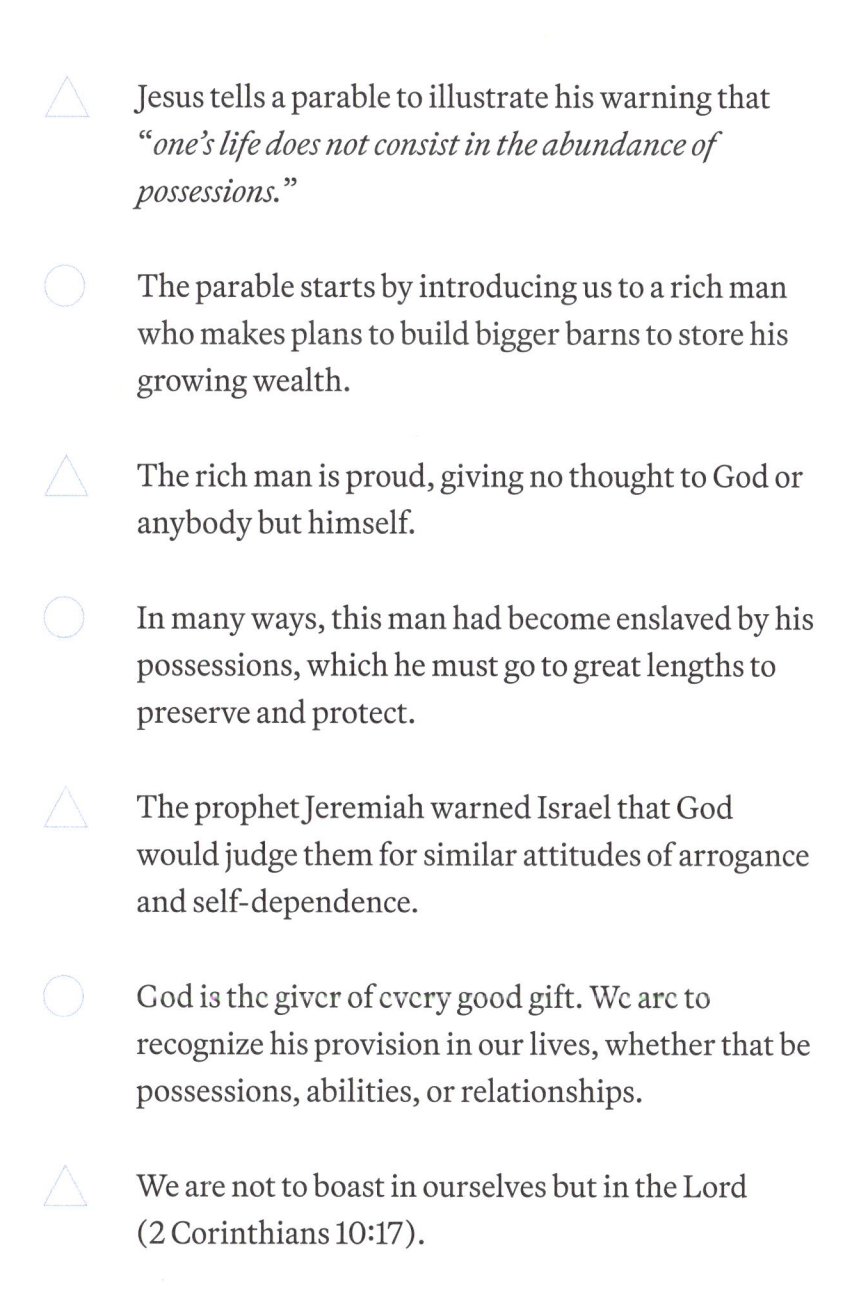

- Jesus tells a parable to illustrate his warning that *"one's life does not consist in the abundance of possessions."*

- The parable starts by introducing us to a rich man who makes plans to build bigger barns to store his growing wealth.

- The rich man is proud, giving no thought to God or anybody but himself.

- In many ways, this man had become enslaved by his possessions, which he must go to great lengths to preserve and protect.

- The prophet Jeremiah warned Israel that God would judge them for similar attitudes of arrogance and self-dependence.

- God is the giver of every good gift. We are to recognize his provision in our lives, whether that be possessions, abilities, or relationships.

- We are not to boast in ourselves but in the Lord (2 Corinthians 10:17).

Reflect

Take a moment to meditate on the following questions:

What have you learned about God from this week's study?

What have you learned about yourself?

Pray

"Merciful and loving Father, forgive me for yielding to things that cannot bring me life. Right now, I confess any prideful attitudes and turn to you for redemption and forgiveness. The abundance of your grace is more than I could ever ask or imagine. Through the Holy Spirit and your Word, teach me to trust your steadfast love, your justice, and your righteousness in my life, so that I may boast in You, and not in the things I own or accomplish. In Jesus' name, Amen."

Practice

Here are a few activities to help guide you as you meditate on this week:

READ — Read and meditate on Jeremiah 9:23-24 each day this week.

WRITE — Write Jeremiah 9:23-24 on a card and carry it with you, or add a reminder in your phone to help you reflect on it daily.

ASK — Ask God how you can come to "understand and know" him more fully.

REFLECT — Reflect on the things that delight the Lord and recall the times you've seen these things in your own life.

CONFESS — Confess to the Lord the times you have boasted in your own abilities, set your hopes on things of this world, or failed to recognize God's love and provision in your life.

> If we confess our sins, he is faithful and just to forgive us our sins and to cleanse us from all unrighteousness.
>
> **1 JOHN 1:9**

JEREMIAH 9:23–24

²³ Thus says the Lord:
"Let not the wise man
boast in his wisdom,
let not the mighty man
boast in his might,
let not the rich man
boast in his riches,
²⁴ but let him who boasts
boast in this,
that he understands and knows me,
that I am the Lord who practices
steadfast love, justice,
and righteousness in the earth.
For in these things I delight,
declares the Lord."

Week 2 — Journal

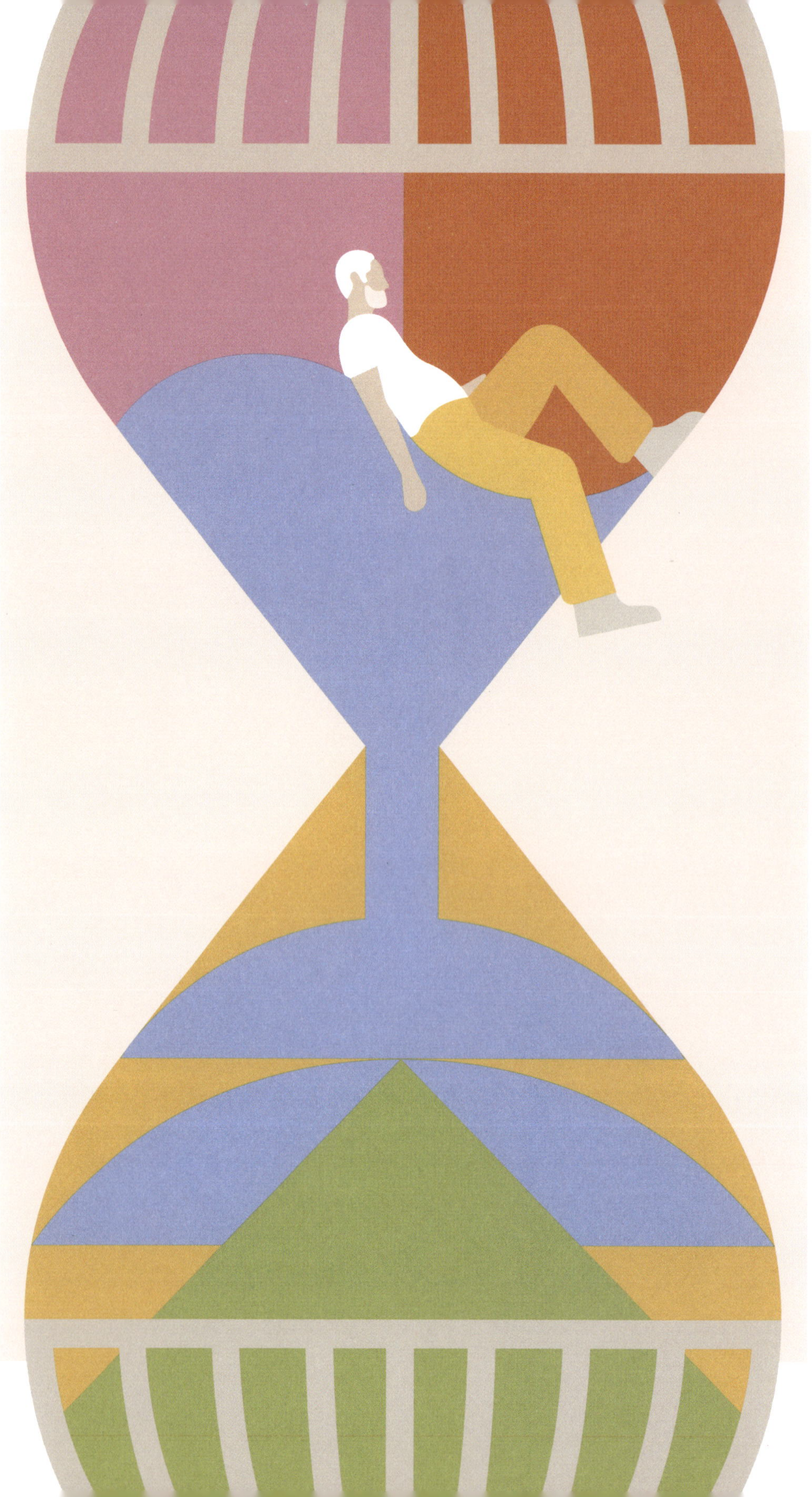

Week 3

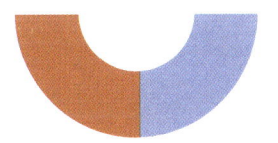

The Uncertainty of Tomorrow

LUKE 12:19–20

TEACHING PASSAGE

¹⁹ "And I will say to my soul, 'Soul, you have ample goods laid up for many years; relax, eat, drink, be merry.'" ²⁰ But God said to him, "Fool! This night your soul is required of you, and the things you have prepared, whose will they be?"

LUKE 12:19–20

Setting the Scene

Earlier in our study, Jesus warned about covetousness in response to a request from a man in the crowd: *"Teacher, tell my brother to divide the inheritance with me."* To illustrate his point, Jesus tells a parable about a rich man with big plans for his burgeoning wealth. In these next verses, Jesus brings the story of the rich fool to its dramatic end.

Every one of us has struggled with greed or covetousness at one time or another. These sins, like every other, separate us from God. The rich man in Jesus' parable isn't just greedy, though. He is also proud, selfish, and idolatrous. This rich man fails to consider God or anyone else when he plans for his wealth, and he expects to perpetuate his comfortable lifestyle without any thought to God's priorities. He is confident in himself and his future of leisure. Tragically arrogant, he fails to anticipate the reality of death, which brings an end to both his accumulation and his future.

Digging Deeper

In Luke 12:18-19, the rich man makes his plans to secure his future, a future powered by his own ingenuity and effort. His expectations are rosy.

> What does he intend to do with his time, once he has "ample goods laid up for many years"?

Again, we see the rich man talking to himself in verse 19, just as he did in verse 17. The word "soul" refers to his essential being, his inner self. He's saying to himself, "I have arrived. Now, it's time to kick back and relax."

It is at this point in verse 20 that God speaks.

> Why do you think God intervenes at this point in the parable?

The Anatomy of a Fool

We don't hear people calling each other "fool" very often nowadays, but in Jesus' time, it was a strong insult, even a curse. Calling someone a fool meant passing judgment on them as godless and unredeemable.[1]

In the Sermon on the Mount, Jesus warned that to call someone a fool in this way would put you in danger of the fires of hell.[2] So, why does God use this language? Consider the fact that God can see into a person's heart. When we call someone a name, we do it based on assumptions and opinion,

---

1   Henry, Matthew. *Commentary on the Whole Bible*: Genesis to Revelation. 1961, p. 1223.

2   Gill, John. *John Gill's Exposition of the Bible*; Matthew 5:22.

not fact. When God calls someone a fool, it's an accurate description based on what the Lord sees inside the person. He is never unjust, but always righteous.

> There is only one lawgiver and judge, he who is able to save and to destroy. But who are you to judge your neighbor?
>
> JAMES 4:12

In Scripture, there are different types of people God calls "fool." One is found in Psalm 14:1, *"The fool says in his heart, 'There is no God.'"* This fool is someone who rejects God's authority and existence from the depths of his heart. A fool of this caliber is not misled, but deliberately rejecting the truth.

Another kind of fool is found in Proverbs 14:9, *"Fools mock at the guilt offering..."* This fool knows the truth about God, and may even claim to worship him, but rejects the idea that sin has consequences. This fool prefers to ignore the need for repentance.

A third kind of fool is one who acts like the rich man in our parable. Fools like this are prepared to secure their own future without considering God. They use their wealth to provide their own security, leisure, and identity without acknowledging any need for God and his grace.

What do these three kinds of fools have in common?

Why does God call the rich man a "fool"?

The rich fool might think he is choosing a path straight to a comfortable retirement, with no worries on the horizon. Evangelist Billy Graham expressed the tragedy of this blindness to sin,

"There is always something pathetic about a man who thinks he is rich when he is actually poor, who thinks he is good when he is actually vile, who thinks he is educated when he is actually illiterate."

This is the basis of the rich man's foolishness—he thinks he is rich, when he is actually poor. He has nobody but himself and his "stuff," and considers that enough to provide a secure and comfortable future. The rich fool becomes blind to God, others, and even his own mortality as he zeroes in on the currency he thinks will satisfy his deepest needs.

The Paradox of Planning

The rich man in our parable develops a great financial plan in his own mind.

Re-read Luke 12:18-19.

> And he said, "I will do this: I will tear down my barns and build larger ones, and there I will store all my grain and my goods. And I will say to my soul, 'Soul, you have ample goods laid up for many years; relax, eat, drink, be merry.'"
>
> LUKE 12:18-19

Write out the rich man's "to do" list, according to this passage.

"There is always something pathetic about a man who thinks he is rich when he is actually poor, who thinks he is good when he is actually vile, who thinks he is educated when he is actually illiterate."

— BILLY GRAHAM

Today, many people consider retirement to be a time to relax and enjoy the fruit of years of hard work. We might even say, like the rich man, "I have ample goods laid up for many years; now I can relax, eat, drink, and be merry."

In what ways are your expectations of "retirement" similar to what the rich man planned in Jesus' parable?

The paradox of planning is this: Good stewardship requires prudent preparation for the future, and yet it's a future we can't either see or control.

God's Word offers a perspective on this paradox. It begins by stating the problem in James 4:13-14.

> Come now, you who say, "Today or tomorrow we will go into such and such a town and spend a year there and trade and make a profit"—yet you do not know what tomorrow will bring. What is your life? For you are a mist that appears for a little time and then vanishes.
>
> JAMES 4:13-14

How is the rich man in Jesus' parable similar to the presumptuous planners in James' example?

Do you think this means we should never make plans? Why or why not?

According to Scripture, when we make plans, we must not neglect the will of God or act as if we're in charge of the results, as did the rich man.

James offers the solution to the paradox of planning:

> Instead you ought to say, "If the Lord wills, we will live and do this or that." As it is, you boast in your arrogance. All such boasting is evil. So whoever knows the right thing to do and fails to do it, for him it is sin.
>
> JAMES 4:15–17

How does James encourage Christians to approach planning for the future?

Seeking God's Will

God's Word reminds us that planning without God in mind is foolish. After all, the Lord both sees and controls the future. According to Proverbs 19:21,

> Many are the plans in the mind of a man, but it is the purpose of the Lord that will stand.
>
> PROVERBS 19:21

Even if our carefully laid plans do not pan out, as children of the King we can rest assured that **his plans** will always succeed. The Christian's desire should be to discover what pleases the Lord, then pursue his purposes with all our heart. Our loving Heavenly Father doesn't leave us in the dark about all this.

We can look to God's Word to find out what pleases him.

> ³⁷ You shall love the Lord your God with all your heart and with all your soul and with all your mind. ³⁸ This is the great and first commandment. ³⁹ And a second is like it: You shall love your neighbor as yourself. ⁴⁰ On these two commandments depend all the Law and the Prophets.
>
> MATTHEW 22:37–40

> He has told you, O man, what is good; and what does the LORD require of you but to do justice, and to love kindness, and to walk humbly with your God?
>
> MICAH 6:8

How could these two passages help shape your financial plans and decisions?

The wisdom of Proverbs 3:5-7 provides us with valuable insight into how we can seek God's will.

> Trust in the LORD with all your heart, and do not lean on your own understanding. In all your ways acknowledge him, and he will make straight your paths. Be not wise in your own eyes; fear the LORD, and turn away from evil.
>
> PROVERBS 3:5-7

List six ways believers can pursue God, according to this scripture passage.

What is the gracious promise found in this passage?

What stands out to you from Proverbs 3-5:7 that may be preventing you from an abundant relationship with God?

When you acknowledge God in all your ways, he will make straight your paths. What do you think that practically looks like when making your financial plans?

Recap

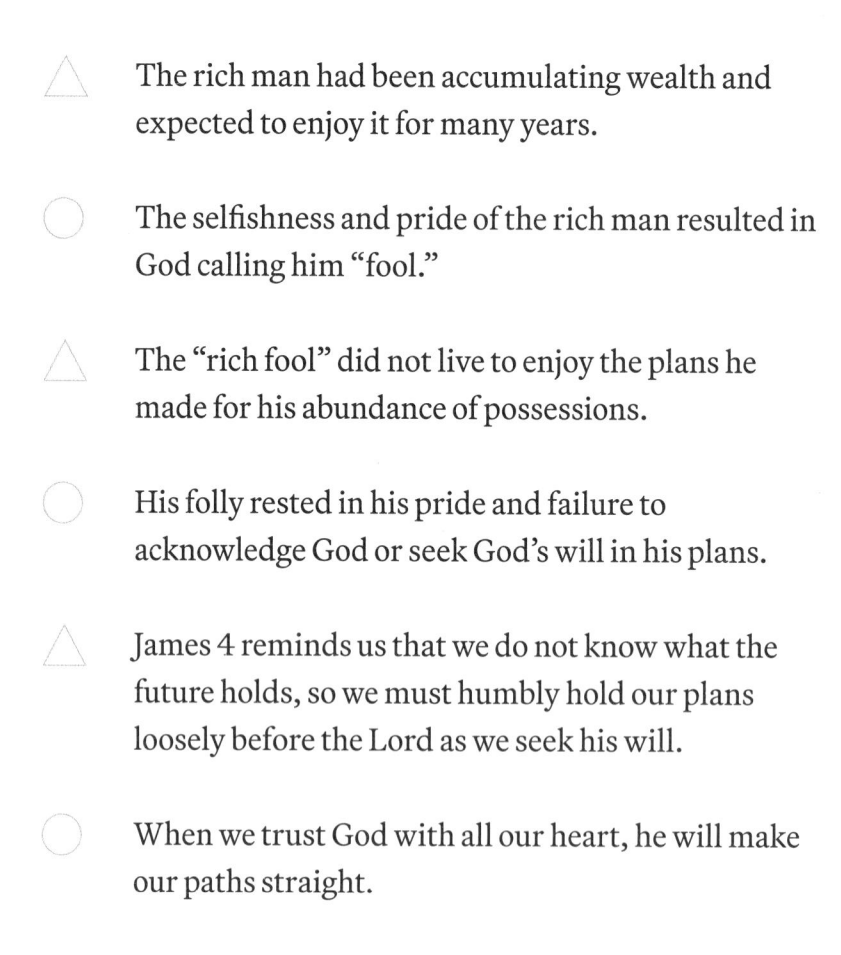

△ The rich man had been accumulating wealth and expected to enjoy it for many years.

○ The selfishness and pride of the rich man resulted in God calling him "fool."

△ The "rich fool" did not live to enjoy the plans he made for his abundance of possessions.

○ His folly rested in his pride and failure to acknowledge God or seek God's will in his plans.

△ James 4 reminds us that we do not know what the future holds, so we must humbly hold our plans loosely before the Lord as we seek his will.

○ When we trust God with all our heart, he will make our paths straight.

Reflect

Take a moment to meditate on the following questions:

What have you learned about God from this week's study?

What have you learned about yourself?

Pray

"Eternal Lord, you are more precious to me than anything else in the world. Forgive me for the times when I put my trust in anything but you. I don't know what tomorrow will bring, but I do know you love me, and I don't need to worry. Lead me in paths of righteousness for your name's sake today, Lord. In Jesus' name I pray, Amen."

Practice

On the following pages, examine your own financial life and consider the ways your finances impact your relationship with God.

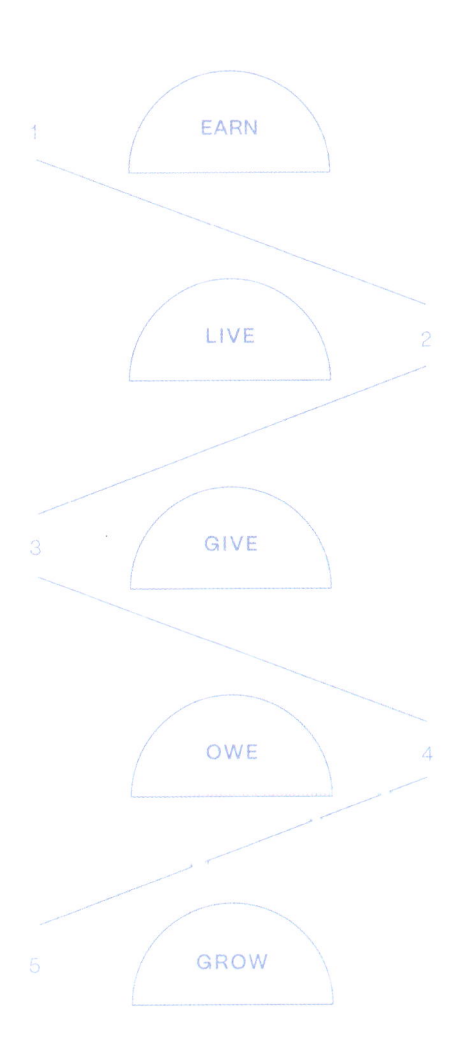

1 EARN

2 LIVE

3 GIVE

4 OWE

5 GROW

EARN

How is your income impacting your identity?

Are you tempted to boast in your own efforts to earn or accumulate money? How can you turn from boasting in self to boasting in the Lord?

Do you trust God as your provider? Why or why not?

LIVE

How can you seek God's will when making lifestyle choices—from big purchases (housing, transportation, vacations) to daily spending decisions?

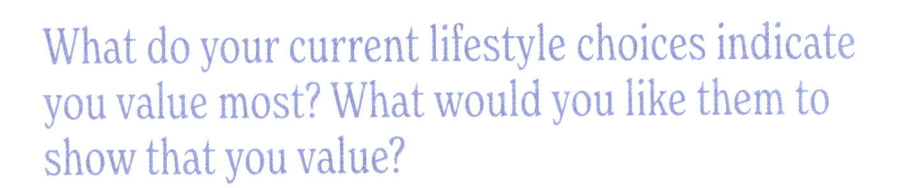

What do your current lifestyle choices indicate you value most? What would you like them to show that you value?

GIVE

What are the motivations behind your giving?

How often do you pray for the Lord's guidance about where and how much to give?

How can your giving be a reflection of our generous God?

OWE

Do you go to God in prayer before taking on debt?

How does debt impact your ability to trust God to provide?

If you are in debt, how are you seeking God's will to help direct you to get out of debt?

GROW

Do you find your security in your financial assets? How can you find your security in the Lord?

Have you sought the Lord's direction to answer the question, "How much is enough?"

How can you align your long-term financial plans with God's will?

PROVERBS 3:5-7

⁵ Trust in the LORD with all your heart, and do not lean on your own understanding. ⁶ In all your ways acknowledge him, and he will make straight your paths. ⁷ Be not wise in your own eyes; fear the LORD, and turn away from evil.

Week 3 — Journal

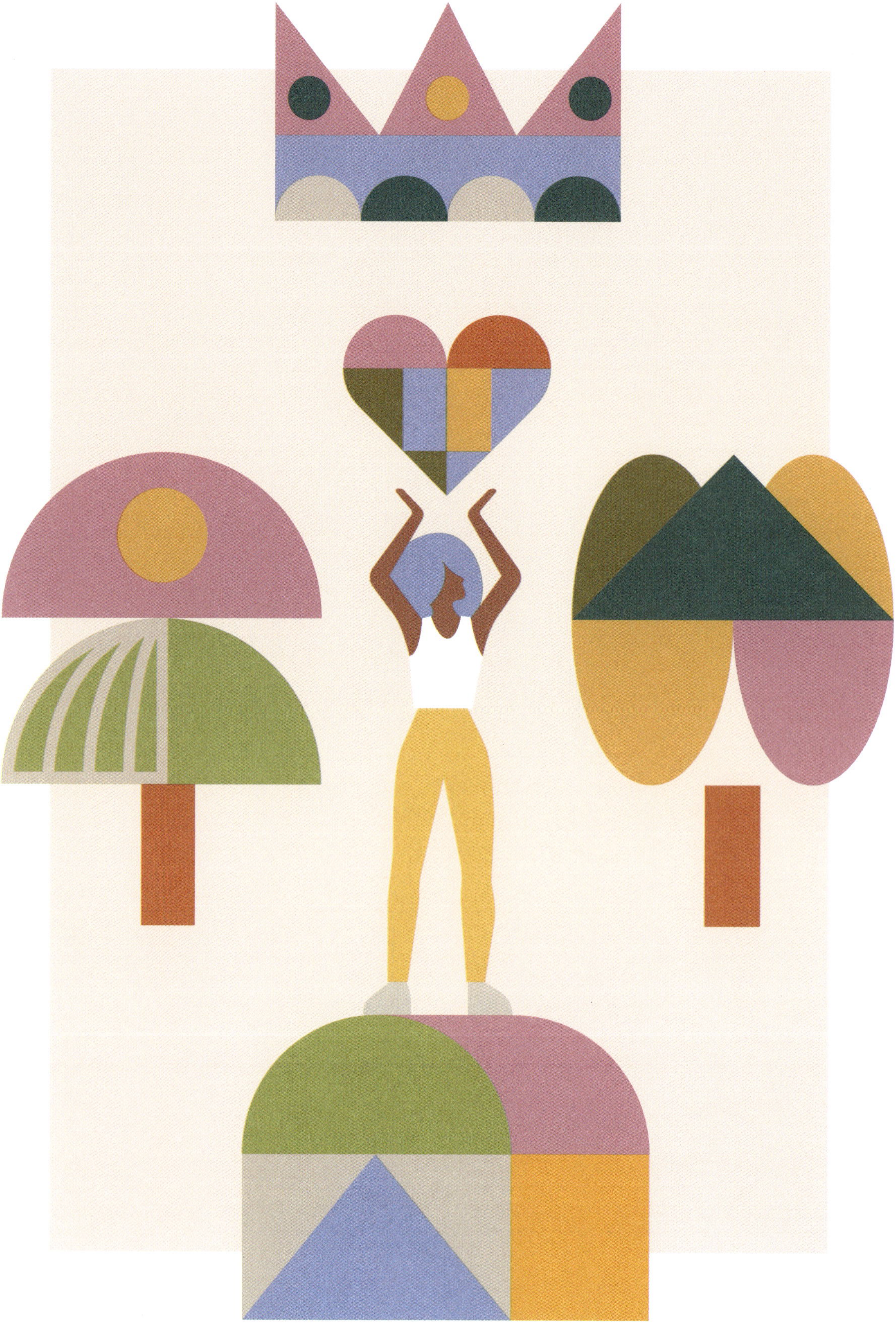

Week 4

Rich Toward God

LUKE 12:21

TEACHING PASSAGE

"So is the one who lays up treasure for himself and is not rich toward God."

LUKE 12:21

Setting the Scene

Jesus wraps up the parable of the rich fool in dramatic fashion. The rich man made his plans but never got to see them carried out. He had focused his time, energy, skills, thoughts, dreams, and plans on financial gain. But in the end, he lost it all. His arrogance and self-glorification were revealed as foolishness when God intervened and his life ended abruptly.

God asked the question, *"The things you have prepared, whose will they be?"* (verse 20), and we also wonder, "Who gets all his stuff?" This returns us to the issue that started it all—a man in the crowd wanting Jesus to mediate a family dispute over inheritance.

In the end, we realize what Jesus is teaching us through this parable: that no inheritance or financial accumulation will fulfill our desires for things only God can supply. Money is transient. God and his ways are eternal.

Now we will zero in on the final verse of this passage, in which Jesus invites us to discover what it means to be "rich toward God."

Digging Deeper

Jesus points to the rich man as an example of a foolish life: *"...one who lays up treasures for himself and is not rich toward God."* The rich man focused his desires on money, possessions, and self-interest instead of the Lord. He had everything in worldly terms he could have dreamed of, but at what cost?

The rich man's life is reminiscent of the question Jesus asks in Matthew 16:26:

> ### What will it profit a man if he gains the whole world and forfeits his soul?
> MATTHEW 16:26

In Luke 12:21 Jesus leaves the inheritance-seeking brother, his followers, and all of us with a critical question: "What does it mean to be rich toward God?" Is the Parable of the Rich Fool simply a call to give away money and possessions, or is Jesus inviting us into something more?

Imperishable Inheritance

Luke 12:13-21 began with a man asking about an inheritance. Jesus, refusing to settle the dispute, saw the real problem at hand. He knew that an inheritance would be a false solution to the heart problem of the questioner, so he took the time to invite the man—and the rest of his followers—into a richer life with God by telling him a stark story about the futile "inheritance" of someone who does not know God.

Jesus calls us to step out of that kind of futility and into a new way of life, focusing our hope on a richer, eternal inheritance. Peter writes about this imperishable inheritance that we have in Christ:

³ Blessed be the God and Father of our Lord Jesus Christ! According to his great mercy, he has caused us to be born again to a living hope through the resurrection of Jesus Christ from the dead, ⁴ **to an inheritance that is imperishable, undefiled, and unfading, kept in heaven for you,** ⁵ who by God's power are being guarded through faith for a salvation ready to be revealed in the last time. ⁶ In this you rejoice, though now for a little while, if necessary, you have been grieved by various trials, ⁷ so that the tested genuineness of your faith—more precious than gold that perishes though it is tested by fire—may be found to result in praise and glory and honor at the revelation of Jesus Christ. ⁸ Though you have not seen him, you love him. Though you do not now see him, you believe in him and rejoice with joy that is inexpressible and filled with glory, ⁹ obtaining the outcome of your faith, the salvation of your souls.

1 PETER 1:3–9

- According to this passage, what is our source of hope?

- Describe the eternal inheritance we have in Christ.

- What is more precious than gold (verse 7)?

- What is the evidence of our faith in the resurrected Christ (verse 8-9)?

Our Ultimate Treasure

In the Parable of the Rich Fool, the words "rich" and "treasure" have both physical and spiritual meanings. On one hand they denote worldly success and prosperity. Their heavenly counterparts are a different matter. When God becomes our heart's treasure, the riches we enjoy are spiritual and eternal. He offers us abundance we cannot find in this world.

> Fear not, little flock, for it is your Father's good pleasure to give you the kingdom. Sell your possessions, and give to the needy. Provide yourselves with moneybags that do not grow old, with a treasure in the heavens that does not fail, where no thief approaches and no moth destroys. **For where your treasure is, there will your heart be also.**
>
> LUKE 12:32–34

The Parable of the Rich Fool reminds us that although we were created with a longing for abundance and life, we often locate our longings in places that can't ultimately satisfy our hearts.

If someone were to look at how you spend your time and money, what would they say you treasure most?

To be clear, the Bible doesn't condemn wealth or possessions or claim that money is evil in itself. All the good gifts God provides are to be received with thanksgiving (1 Timothy 4:4). But problems arise when we love the creation more than the Creator. Author Paul David Tripp writes:

"What the Bible clearly teaches is that when functional, life-shaping love for money and what it allows you to acquire and enjoy squeezes out of your heart the functional, life-shaping love for God that was designed to be the organizing principle of your life, then you are a person in deep spiritual trouble...Money is one of God's good creations, but this good thing becomes a bad thing for you when it becomes a ruling thing. You simply cannot serve the King of kings and have acquisition of wealth as the organizing dream of your heart."[1]

If God is our treasure, our life will reflect God's character to the world. As image-bearers of a relational and generous God, one beautiful and tangible way we exhibit our love for God is through our financial decisions.

We are called to be a light to the world (Matthew 5:14) and as such, our finances can be a powerful testimony of our faith in Jesus. The ways we earn money, our lifestyle, generosity, financial priorities, and perspective of money and possessions become a reflection of who we are in Christ.

When our abundance is found in the person of Jesus, we become open-handed with our finances as we seek his kingdom and his righteousness. Generosity is no longer something we do out of obligation or to be seen by others, but it becomes something that flows out of a grateful heart that treasures God and longs to see others come to know and love Him.

How could the rich man have avoided being called a "fool" at the end of his life?

---

[1] Tripp, Paul David. *Sex and Money* (p. 164). Crossway.

"Money is one of God's good creations, but this good thing becomes a bad thing for you when it becomes a ruling thing."

— PAUL DAVID TRIPP

In the Parable of the Rich Fool, Jesus is inviting us to so much more than giving money or possessions away. He's calling us to store up treasures in heaven by giving our heart to him and making God our riches. Pastor and Author John Piper puts it this way:

*"'Rich toward God' means moving toward God as our riches. 'Rich toward God' means counting God greater riches than anything on the earth. 'Rich toward God' means **using earthly riches to show how much you value God**."*

Jesus is inviting you to make him the desire of your heart, every moment of every day. Will you surrender your life, plans, and finances to him? Will you allow him to be your ultimate treasure?

In your own words, what does it mean to be rich toward God?

How will you be rich toward God?

Recap

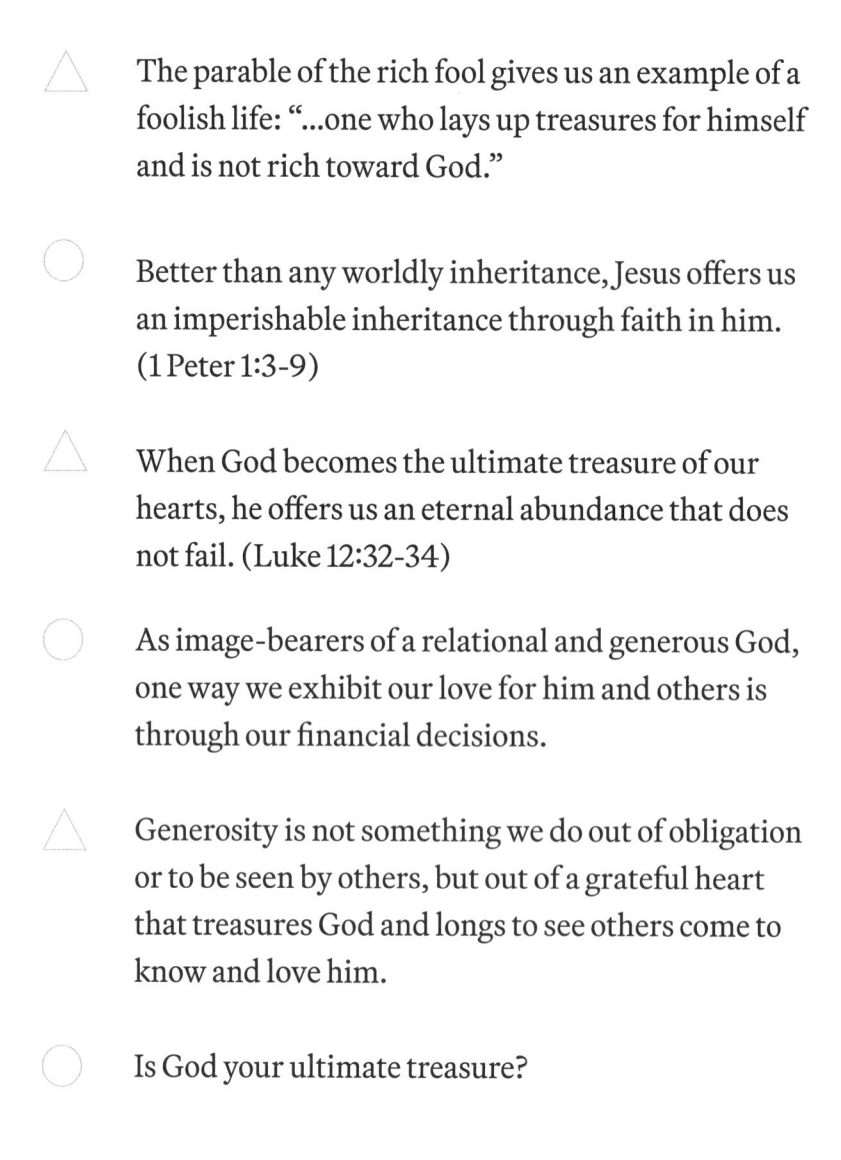

△ The parable of the rich fool gives us an example of a foolish life: "...one who lays up treasures for himself and is not rich toward God."

○ Better than any worldly inheritance, Jesus offers us an imperishable inheritance through faith in him. (1 Peter 1:3-9)

△ When God becomes the ultimate treasure of our hearts, he offers us an eternal abundance that does not fail. (Luke 12:32-34)

○ As image-bearers of a relational and generous God, one way we exhibit our love for him and others is through our financial decisions.

△ Generosity is not something we do out of obligation or to be seen by others, but out of a grateful heart that treasures God and longs to see others come to know and love him.

○ Is God your ultimate treasure?

Reflect

Take a moment to meditate on
the following questions:

What have you learned about God from this week's study?

What have you learned about yourself?

Pray

"Heavenly Father, my heart's desire is to be rich toward you, putting you first in everything, including my finances. Forgive me for allowing anything other than you to rule and reign in my life. Teach me by your Holy Spirit to fill my mind and heart with whatever is true, honorable, just, pure, lovely, commendable, excellent, and praiseworthy. Help me to be a vessel to impact the Kingdom, in my finances, and through other opportunities to love as you love. Make me more like Jesus every day. Amen."

Practice

Here are ways you can practice being rich toward God.

As you read each scripture, ask the Lord to show you how to put the spiritual disciplines into practice. Keep a record of your journey with the Lord, to remember his faithfulness.

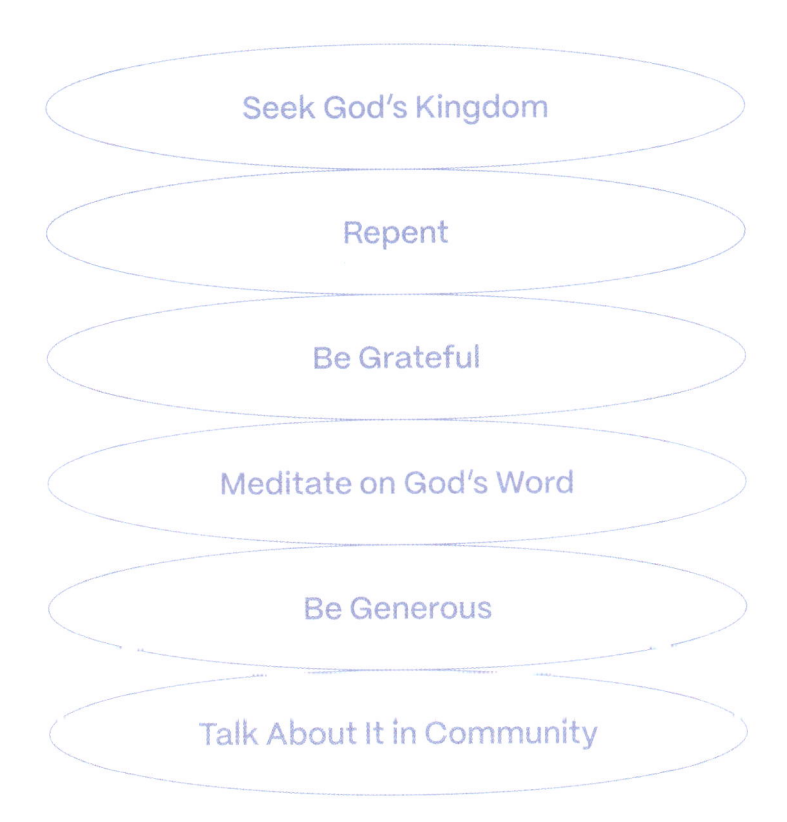

- Seek God's Kingdom
- Repent
- Be Grateful
- Meditate on God's Word
- Be Generous
- Talk About It in Community

Seek God's Kingdom

> Therefore do not be anxious, saying, "What shall we eat?" or "What shall we drink?" or "What shall we wear?" For the Gentiles seek after all these things, and your heavenly Father knows that you need them all. **But seek first the kingdom of God and his righteousness, and all these things will be added to you.**
>
> MATTHEW 6:31–33

Ask God to reveal the ways in which you are seeking your kingdom instead of his. Ask him to give you strength by his Holy Spirit to *"seek first the kingdom of God and his righteousness."*

Are you seeking your kingdom instead of God's? If so, how can you put his kingdom first?

Repent

> Whoever conceals his transgressions will not prosper, but he who confesses and forsakes them will obtain mercy.
>
> PROVERBS 28:13

Repentance is the act of turning away from sin and toward God. Ask God's forgiveness for when you put anything ahead of him in your life and ask him to graciously make him your sole treasure.

Is there anything you put above the Lord that you need to repent of?

Be Grateful

> We give thanks to you, O God; we give thanks, for your name is near. We recount your wondrous deeds.
>
> **PSALM 75:1**

Develop a rhythm of gratitude by regularly reflecting on and writing down what you are thankful for. Remember the times you've seen God's grace and mercy in your life!

What are you most thankful for?

Meditate on God's Word

> This Book of the Law shall not depart from your mouth, but you shall meditate on it day and night, so that you may be careful to do according to all that is written in it. For then you will make your way prosperous, and then you will have good success.
>
> JOSHUA 1:8

Spend time in the Word to grow in your relationship with God and to discern his will for all areas of your life, including your financial decisions and choices.

What are some practical ways you can spend more time with God?

Be Generous

> Do not neglect to do good and to share what you have, for such sacrifices are pleasing to God.
>
> **HEBREWS 13:16**

What time, talents, and treasures has God entrusted to you? Respond to the generosity of God by cultivating a lifestyle of generosity toward others.

What time, talents, and treasures has God entrusted to you that you might share with others?

Talk About It in Community

> Therefore encourage one another and build one another up, just as you are doing.
>
> **1 THESSALONIANS 5:11**

Share what you've learned through this study of God's Word with friends and family, or consider leading a small group at church.

Is there anyone that God has highlighted to you that would benefit from this study?

LUKE 12:32–34

³² "Fear not, little flock, for it is your Father's good pleasure to give you the kingdom. ³³ Sell your possessions, and give to the needy. Provide yourselves with moneybags that do not grow old, with a treasure in the heavens that does not fail, where no thief approaches and no moth destroys. ³⁴ For where your treasure is, there will your heart be also."